NOTIONS

First published in 2018 by
The Dedalus Press
13 Moyclare Road
Baldoyle
Dublin D13 K1C2
Ireland

www.**dedaluspress**.com

ISBN 978 1 910251 42 3 HB
ISBN 978 1 910251 41 6 PB

Dedalus Press titles are represented in the UK by
Inpress Books, www.inpressbooks.co.uk.

Cover painting: 'Walking Man' by Basil Blackshaw
Oil on canvas, 24 x 40 in (61 x 102 cm)
By kind permission of the artist's estate

The Dedalus Press receives financial assistance from
The Arts Council / An Chomhairle Ealaíon.

NOTIONS

JOHN KELLY

DEDALUS PRESS

ACKNOWLEDGEMENTS

My thanks to the Estate of Basil Blackshaw for kind permission to use *Walking Man* on the cover.

A number of these poems have previously appeared in various literary journals. I'm grateful to the editors of *Poetry Ireland Review, The Well Review, Winter Papers, Banshee, The Irish Times, The Irish Review* and *Oxford Magazine*. 'The Lenin Mausoleum' first appeared in *The Honest Ulsterman*, ed. Frank Ormsby (1988), *The New Younger Irish Poets,* ed. Gerald Dawe (Blackstaff Press, 1991) and *Trio 7* (Blackstaff Press, 1992).

I'd like to acknowledge the following friends and co-conspirators who counselled, encouraged and said the kind word at the crucial time – Gerard Smyth, Doireann Ní Ghríofa, Katie Donovan, Maria Johnston, Declan MacManus, Bernard O'Donoghue, Theo Dorgan, Marina Carr, Des Lally, Tom Dillon, Sinéad Gleeson, Séamas MacAnnaidh, Eric Mingus, Andrew Fitzsimons, Medbh McGuckian, Trevor Griffiths, David Hammond, Seamus Heaney & Dennis O'Driscoll.

My deepest gratitude to my editor Pat Boran for his support, care and attention in the making of this book.

CONTENTS

≈

The Small Things / 9

– 1 –

– 2 –

– 3 –

∿

in memory of my parents
Lily Kennedy & Tommy Kelly

The Small Things

I put my shoulder out, swimming with the kids,
bluffing the backstroke in a gloopy Spanish pool,
and, for a year or more, could hardly lift a cup.

A torn rotator cuff. Chiros, physios, osteos
all had a go, till I fixed it myself in the gym,
working it sideways, with the lightest weight there was.

This morning, risking it again, with presses,
ring-rows, curls, I sense
the cranky silver arm of a slot machine,

and I'm back in Bundoran in my anorak,
in the racket-flash of the amusement arcade.
Just my mother and me.

She wears a yellow headscarf.
Lipstick. The holiday drizzle
is still on her cheek.

When three chopped watermelons thud into place
the bells ring out. A jackpot clatter
as still-warm coins return to us in spills.

We buy chicken and chips with our winnings.
She loves her silver pot of tea.
Fizzy orange with a straw for me.

1

Ornithology

That first connection to the open world
was *The Ladybird Book of Garden Birds.*

The Finches lived on Derrin Road.
The Martins lived beside the Swifts

on Corban Avenue.
Of course, I didn't know that Corbin

came from *corvus*, meaning crow.
(That was Harry Martin. Tommy Swift.)

And wasn't there a Dr. Crane
who was, I think, a chiropodist?

So at the kitchen window
the ornithology began –

chaffinch, sparrow, starling,
collared dove and wren.

But that bullfinch pair
was the first and proper sign

that wondrous things might exist
in a life like mine.

How had I never seen those blacks and reds
before? How could I have missed

a snow-white blackbird
by the coal-shed door?

In Lieu

My football bag was blue.
It was often searched
in case there was a bomb in it
in lieu of boots.
Or an Armalite in lieu of togs,
or gelignite in lieu of Brut,
or the names of likely targets
on some incriminating list
in lieu of Nualas and Siobháns
who might agree,
in lieu of nothing else to do,
to kissing at The Ritz.

Control Zone

The town was blocked at either end,
the customary chokehold
for northern streets all set for bombs.

And I was staring at my feet
as I passed the watching cops,
Sten guns wilting by the flower shop.

Or the Brits decked out in nets and twigs,
perhaps a slowing unmarked car,
or some loaded tribal dig from the passing UDR.

And after football at the Complex (Christ!)
I'd walk home through the town
and my bag was rifled through again

in case it carried anything incendiary
bar an inky *NME* –
all this before they'd even let me see

the racks of singles and LPs in Woolworths.
Oliver's Army, Guns of Brixton.
And this when a Chinese restaurant

was as rare as *Chinese Rocks.*
God Save the Queen, It's Gonna Happen! –
a black armband on Top of the Pops.

Antonyms

i.m. David Hammond

Column after column we learned by rote
the otherness of things.

Not like tables or the spelling book
this exercise was new,

you had to boomerang the word
and hope it glanced precisely in another place,

came back with an opposite no less –
some other meaning clinging to its curves.

The word reminded me of Anthony (of Padua)
who preached theology to fish,

patron of the lost thing, who found for me
a faulty boomerang in the hedge across the stream.

Or *antiphon* or *antelope* or *Antioch*,
ancient city of God-knows-where.

Was it Greek perhaps or Biblical?
Paul and the Corinthians?

Or something else entirely?
Odysseus? Aladdin? Sinbad the Sailor?

On Air

On Thursday nights the siren went,
a weekly drill for firemen
as we watched *Dad's Army* on the BBC.

It was an old, prolonged lament
and had we lived in Germany in 1942 –
in Essen, Bremen or Cologne –

we might have taken it
for the thousand-bomber raid:
death-laden Lancasters,

Whitleys, Wellingtons,
all heading for the Rhine,
a grim migration, top secret

but almost audible on air
until the head-phoned engineer,
picking up the distant drone,

shut the outside broadcast down –
Beatrice Harrison playing
Songs My Mother Taught Me

in a Surrey garden,
caressing her cello near the trees,
accompanied by nightingales.

Goal of the Season

for Oscar

A goal kick plummets from the sky.
You trap its thud so solidly
and take the sudden measure of it all.

And with your boot so firmly on the ball
you might have stood imperious then,
like Franz "Der Kaiser" Beckenbauer,

an emperor before your time, son,
when West Germany was the thing,
but not at all. You put the head down and away!

Past one, past two, past three,
(Oh, the rhythms of our own self-commentary)
and you are through on goal.

Their frantic little keeper, gloved and brave,
like Dino Zoff comes off his line,
but with a striker's hoodwink eyes

you send him left to nothingness
(by which I mean the other way)
and bury it so casually. *One-Nil!*

And when you turn, your arms spread wide
like a crooner or a saint,
the very first swallow of 2016

begins to loop above your head,
as if anointing you
and eyeing me.

For I'm the age to be relieved
to see them back,
and you already on your way.

Up the line like Cruyff –
the skinny run, the swerving dip,
the dink, the jink, the little skip.

Away to Kilnamanagh,
the M50 roaring
on the far side of the pitch.

Cabal

Where'd Maguire get the word *cabal?*
Was it *Look and Learn?* Or something on the BBC?
But I recall he used it in a composition once,
struck, he said, by the Hebrew etymology.

Did he know, I wonder, what occult overtones there were?
Quabalah? The Rosy Cross? The Golden Dawn?
He said he was thinking more of Charles II's Ministry –
Clifford, Arlington, Buckingham,

Ashley, Lauderdale – CABAL – a coincidental acronym.
In any case, the master flashed the fountain pen
and scored it out. There's no such word, he said,
and marked Maguire down as one to be discouraged,

disparaged in the staff room with the rest.
Making up words! Whatever next?
Then he'd smoke and play his cards –
a secret society, shuffling its regrets.

Haydn's Skull

When Haydn's skull was robbed from the ground, a phrenologist
found
the musical bump to be very large and very round.

The otherwise smooth and yellow dome went to an tUasal Rosenbaum,
secretary to Esterházy – *der Schutzpatron* – who sent the relic home

to Haydn's wife, who put it in a bell-jar to be the life
and soul of grand soirées of musical delight.

After that, a quiet spell with Miss Nan Galligan in Sundays Well
who wanted to but wouldn't tell –

not even to her greatest star – that the Totenkopf in her black armoire
was pleased its pupil Ludwig had gone far.

In the end she left it to the local priest, who sold it but was fleeced
by an antiques dealer from Rathgar, though at least

it ended up in Dublin, where Britton from the Museum,
well aquainted with the skull's *Te Deum,*

began conducting his enquiries, noting down assorted stories
and visiting, on Ailesbury Road, the diplomatic dignatories

of Österreich. And so to the Musikverein
where it would silently remain until 1954 when

solemnly they put it back in Eisenstadt
where the body waited in the plot.

Or so they say because one day when we were playing
football at the so-called seminary, à la GAA,

I climbed high into the blue and caught the slippy skull
that flew and, risking total ridicule,

I stopped the game and stood my ground when I found
the musical bump to be very large and very round.

Give it! Give it! Pass! They shouted.
But this was Papa Haydn's skull! Undoubtedly

the very one! I held it tight against my chest,
the other boys were not impressed, the Principal blessed

himself and ordered everybody off the field.
But kneeling now I would not yield 'til I was hauled

away, the Schädel in my frantic grasp. Until today,
at last, I passed the thing away. Away from me to Austria.

A skull, hand-passed, for fleeter boys than me to chase.
Not anyplace. But into space.

The Lenin Mausoleum

If this was the clean, green morgue
of the Erne Hospital
or a prayerful candled bedroom
in a curtained council house,
I'd touch his head and bless myself
and hope he was in Heaven.

I'd shake hands with the family
and wait with solemn men
in a hallway he'd papered just
the week before. *Hard on the wife ...*
Looks well, doesn't he? That week
in Bundoran done him the world of good ...

In Moscow, I pass on through respectfully,
checking the hands for Rosary beads,
alert in case he moves. And out
the back I offer my condolences
with the only words I know –
Glasnost. Vodka. Kalashnikov.

Katya

Confounded by the underground,
the metaphysics of Cyrillic,
I took her by the hand
and she led me, light-wards, to the street.

Her ideal, she said, was Tony Curtis
but, courteous to a fault,
from a Baltic village on the Gulf,
she fed me vodka made with birch sap

and we were happy for a month
behind the fading ginger curtains
of the spacious Hotel Cosmos
in The Soviet Union – as was – in 1985.

Evenings in Pushkin Square,
we were well observed and overheard
by that sulky lad who was always there
in a leather coat that shone like coal –

at least until I collared him
up against the hotel door
and wound him up
with talk of Boney M and Rasputin

and the fading ginger curtains
of the Hotel Killyhevlin
and me out gallivantin'
as lonely as a dog.

Then I never saw Katya again.
She could be in Heaven or Helsinki
or the gangster coast of Spain
and I could be thinking of her always

as the one who got away.
But just today I saw our minder
on the BBC. The G8 Summit,
and Putin (ex-KGB)

was swimming
in a warm Fermanagh lake
and still as sulky as a trout, crawling
about through eels and bream and pike,

tailed at quite some distance
by the same beluga sturgeon
I caught one bright May morning
and very carefully put back.

The Gaeltacht

At the very top of Errigal,
along with Mags O'Neill and Anne-Marie
and Fearghal Short and Deirdre Long,
there was Nadia Jane Gilgunn,
a wondrous blonde from Iúr Cinn Trá
with visible crimson bra straps
and a Lemon Fanta tongue.

And, against all odds, she was the one
who froze on the ridge of One Man's Pass.
There at the clouded pinnacle,
stricken by the magical,
by space, and possibility perhaps,
she turned, in tears, to gleaming quartz
as she straddled, gripped and clung.

Oboli

In a campsite in a rocky field
the ghosts of two Greek women.

They might have been from any time,
but from their jewellery,

from the texture of their hair,
I'd guess the Sixties or the Trojan Wars.

I was sleeping in the air that night,
my dream destroyed by sex-noise –

dark sobbing in the tents and drunken shouts
that woke me in the dream itself,

the ghosts of two Greek women,
silver flashing in their mouths.

Blue Lightning

for Catherine

Such blessings in a storm.
Like aurora borealis or shooting stars,
there's a certain fortune in where we are.

The sky so infinite and pitch
flashed suddenly tonight and caught
two otters in surprise daylight

on Machaire Rabhartaigh.
This morning's tracks appeared again –
our tideline footprints pearled with hail.

I talk of rubber soles.
How I'm earthed like a heron
or a telegraph pole.

Halloween Owl

Before the Gaelic pitch was a Gaelic pitch,
it was a pitch-black hole full of every frog and vole
that ever plashed in moonlit pools.

I can't be sure it was an owl
but, one night, late, already scared,
I saw the false-face tilted down.

Cailleach Oíche. Hag of Night.
Gloom-bird to the poet Keats,
and tonight I saw it on my Dublin street.

It's a foolish man believes in omens,
but like a decent Roman I should have nailed it to the door,
a wreath to ward against the meaning of itself.

I took it for that childhood bird,
not so much for what it was
as for the utter nothingness I heard.

2

Oljato-Monument Valley

I'm eating breakfast at the window –
chili beans and frybread –

when a woman with a beehive
advances to the vista,

grunts hard and says,
It's nothin' but a buncha rocks.

She sits beside me and orders eggs.
I'm Swiss-German-Scotch, I wanna say,

but she isn't long in going away
when I call her pilgrim,

toast Chief Manuelito of the Navajo
and tell her that where I come from

when we play cowboys and Indians
I'm always the Indian. Always.

That my heroes are Crazy Horse,
Rain-In-The-Face, Geronimo …

Lighting a Candle. St. Louis Cathedral, New Orleans

I was there that day in Hanly's Dog Pit,
back in 1869 (or thereabouts),

and Hanly's dog was Cabbage.
The other belonged to Dan O'Neil

who owned the Amsterdam Dance-House
on Gallatin Street.

And many's a time
I was in Bill Swan's too,

The Fireproof Coffee-House on Levee.
(Oh, beware the Live Oak Boys!)

And in the same man's saloon on Peters
and Esplanade for the rat-killing match

that Sunday afternoon in March
when a dog called Modoc killed thirty-six rats

in two minutes and fifty-eight seconds flat.
It cost me 50 cents to get in.

And I was in The House of Rest for Weary Boatmen,
and Mother Colby's Sure Enuf Hotel,

and Archie Murphy's Dance-House
with Delia Swift (call her Bridget Fury)

and I know for a fact
that America Williams and Ellen Collins

were there with Bricktop Jackson
when she knifed that man in Siedendahls.

That same year of '69, I was at the lake chapel
for the last ever ceremony of Marie Laveau –

torn dresses, torches,
a basket of snakes.

And look at her now at the altar rails,
three Guinea peppers in her mouth.

She was seventy-five (or thereabouts)
when she came to see me in the Parish Prison.

On an altar made of boxes
she placed a statue of the Virgin.

She prayed with me.
She brought me gumbo and fried fish.

An Old Woman in Donegal

I asked for the name of the bird
that had landed between us

and was sitting there, pernickety
on a rock, its chipping song

the master's *déan deifir!*
the quizmaster's *hurry up!*

Not the wheatear, I was sure –
the white-arse, *witstaart,*

le petit cul-blanc.
So a bunting perhaps?

A redstart?
Either that

or some exotic class
of Saxicola windblown chat?

But what I wanted
was the Irish word –

Earrdheargán,
Gealóg, Caislín Cloch.

It is, she said, an air-bird.
And left it at that.

Like in Monument Valley
when I asked a Navajo

called Gerald
what he was really called.

And what would be the proper name
for John Ford Point.

54ᵀʰ Street. Above The Oyster Bar

i.m. William Cole

This was the Blizzard of '96
and I was holding tight to a walking stick
that once belonged to O'Donovan Rossa.

I was with the Fenian's grandson, Bill,
editor, poet, anthologist, still
sticking to his literary guns –

James Baldwin, ten years dead,
being one. Electric, he always said,
the smartest man I ever met,

who often sat in the very chair
where I'd been sipping Bloody Marys
from far too early in the day.

Then Alfred Willmore from Kensal Green
began declaiming from an old LP
about the man the English called O'Dynamite,

a man who might have been all ears
to hear Mac Liammóir as Pádraig Pearse
reinstall him in a drift of Midtown snow.

I sit and hold on to the cane
like some Broadway entertainer
waiting in the wings

and from the window looking south
I can see the very movie house
where *Another Country* begins.

Chairman of The Board of Governors

for Paul Brady at 70

He was "out here" to inspect the place –
this far-flung region, the wee broadcasting bothy
beyond the Irish Sea.

But the mandarin ducks of the Belfast BBC
were none too pleased when Lord Marmaduke
made a B-line for me,

taking his patrician ease
in the gloom of Studio 3 where,
as it just so happened,

I was playing *Aura Lee*
as sung by The Shelton Brothers,
a song from the American Civil War

a.k.a *The Maid With Golden Hair* –
the very same tune as *Love Me Tender*
as sung by (saving your presence) the King

and by Freddy Fender too –
just the sort of thing that turned
the ducks and drakes against me in my youth:

that fellow Kelly with his music and his facts,
acting the hapless culchie
when it suits.

Now, Marmaduke Hussey (Dukey to his chums)
was Rugby, Oxford, Grenadier Guards,
not the Fermanagh sept at all,

for that crowd – Ó hEodhasa –
were Maguire's bards,
their English spelling loose and lazy.

No, this man Hussey
was the Norman line instead –
as in Dingle, Fortress of the Husseys,

Daingean Uí Chúis.
So quite amazing, in this way,
to encounter Monsieur de Houssaye.

And what's more his wife was Woman of the Bedchamber
to the Queen. And though I let the matter lie
I could hardly deny that our little chat

had put me closer to the throne
than the likes of me had ever been
since Hugh O'Neill, Earl of Tyrone

(whose bones are lying out in Rome)
was ducking and diving in Greenwich
with the Virgin Queen (as she was known).

And when *Aura Lee* was over I put on another song,
Ponchartrain as sung by Paul,
then *Arthur McBride* as taught to Bob,

the chords passed on at Slane
from Strabane to Minnesota. And all the time
the mandarins had no iota what was going on.

They couldn't hear a word of what we said
and were a-feared that I might spill the beans
or drop a hint or, worse again,

drop them in it
by saying something ill-advised
or offensively uncouth,

some muttered local idiom perhaps,
some reference to *The Iliad, The Upanishads, The Táin,*
the Cumberland, the Mississippi or the Boyne.

But we talked instead about the Civil War
and I mentioned Thomas Francis Meagher
(pronounce it Marr),

Young Irelander who escaped Tasmania
and made it as far as America
to command the Fighting 69th

New York Militia.
Bull Run, Fair Oaks, Fredericksburg.
A Yankee General born in Waterford

on the site of the Granville Hotel.
Drowned in the Missoura, maybe murdered?
Nobody can tell for sure. Not anymore.

And so we nattered on, just me and Duke.
And the suits couldn't bear to look
at anything but their shoes.

And Hussey never mentioned –
though I already knew –
that he had lost a leg at Anzio.

Or rather, by an Axis doctor
it was amputated
and then he was repatriated

to the poor, unfortunate
management classes,
the all-go faux aristocratics,

footering lamentably
with newspapers and broadcasters
but we were cordial even so.

And he was charmed, I think,
to meet the native me. English-speaking
and educated (to a degree),

who had heard of Vicksburg
and Manassas
and told the most peculiar tales

of bards and earls.
And one man in particular –
Have a go, Dukey! – Eochaidh Ó hEodhasa

writing during the Nine Years War:
cúirt 'na doighir, ní díoth nua,
críoch gan oighir, gan iarmhua.

John McGahern's Funeral

Was it Dromod or Rooskey
where the people waiting for the parade
got our flow of Dublin cars instead,
and the people waiting for the hearse
got the foundered marching band?
A dozen crimson melodeons in the rain.
Or was it Ballinamore or Russell Square?
The first of April anyway.
A feis and a funeral on the one day.

The Heavens opened at the church itself,
and caught off-guard by seven priests,
the Rosary – the whole thing as I recall –
and by Hammond, Heaney, Friel
up against the kind of gable wall
you'd hang your crutches on,
I listened in as neighbouring men
with reddened cheeks stepped up
and made the final job complete.
The scrape and thud of Aughawillan clay.
That breath I took before I drove away.

10 January 2016

There was a man who used to cut the grass.
He used a scythe, the snaking shaft of it,
the sned – just right for swivel and for sweep.

A blade so sharp, they said,
it would cut wool floating down a stream.
And tonight I dreamed that man again.

Corrigan or Kerrigan – I forget his name –
but he cut a swathe. He cleared a path.
I saw the frogs, the twitching leveret,

the grasshoppers in splashes.
Then the sudden tilt in everything –
and everything collapses.

In The National Gallery, Oslo

1.

Full of coffee and sunshine I went to see *Skrik*.
A scream passing through nature, the diary said,
and clouds the colour of actual blood.

I was lured by its celebrity, its mystery,
to be able to say that I'd seen it
the next time I landed in Carlingfjord or Killary,

but another painting altogether –
Self-Portrait, Spanish Influenza –
was the one that shook and winded me.

2.

Paddy Kelly lived in Jarrow.
He was an uncle of my father's, a sailor,
and the celebrated hero of many family yarns.

He played the harmonica and once,
for the laugh, he shot the brass knobs
off the end of his bed, then lay back down and slept.

He sailed with the Convoys. At Cape Spartivento
he fired a shell straight up in the air
and shelled his own ship.

He made a radio from a matchbox.
On letters home the address evolved
from Frith's Alley to Frith Avenue.

3.

Was Paddy with the Arctic Convoys too?
I can't be sure. But Kristiania Fjord was just across the floor.
And that famous screaming figure –

man, woman, neither – in tempera and crayon.
I could draw no conclusion, at least not a new one
and, in any case, I was halted there alone

before *Self-Portrait, Spanish Influenza*. 1919.
Oil on canvas, late-phase Munch.
Colourful, raw and roughly done.

The artist in a wicker chair, the gown and blanket,
the open mouth, the eyeless stare. The stench
of yellow poison throughout the wooden house.

I felt again the childhood terror of an unmade double bed.
Paddy orphaned. Spanish Flu. Mother and father dead.
Buried together on the very same day.

P.J. Clarke's

Midtown in a blizzard,
the last of the snowbound strays,
I'm down the back, beside the jukebox, nursing a JD
and listening to Lady Day
whispering (as Frank O'Hara said)
along the keyboard to Mal Waldron.

The bartender sighs, looks over his glasses,
smoothing the woodwork with a cloth.
And just as I call for another Jack
the purple sky turns all magnesium flash
and, not for the first time, in walks Frank Sinatra –
a small, hard snowball in a muscled testudo of goons.

The record jumps. The bartender stops.
But I sit my ground when the huddle breaks
and Frank is loosed, a face on him that would turn milk.
He clocks me right away,
Lonesome Keeper of the Condiments,
Curate of the Heavy Shot Glass.

But I nod to nothing as he passes me by,
into the back room where the ghosts of women
with beehive hair are laughing hard
and waiting for the word,
for some decisive flash of blue.
I return to the jukebox. Put Billie on again.

And that's when Mr. Sinatra
appears suddenly at my elbow,
as if to tell me some half-a-gangster news,

and in the clearest voice he says to me,
You know, kid, Lady was the best.
She walked sideways, she talked sideways
and she sang sideways.

To this day, I still don't know
what, if anything, he meant by that.
But as I settle up that night
I send a JD to the back room.
Then, shoulders hunched against the cold,
I step soft into 3rd Avenue and snow.

The city is empty. Sepia. Tranquilized.
I stand shin-deep with fifty-something blocks to go,
and all I can hear are the fumes of my own breath
and the whiskey's throbbing burn.
I wonder am I wrong to call them goons.
I wonder am I lonely here. Or just, contentedly, alone.

Gin

Measure by measure, as if there's love in it,
he builds himself a drink. If he has it,
he'll add a good vermouth.

In the lamplight he speaks to molecules
of juniper, coriander, liquorice
and grains of paradise,

and laments the Raj, the Famine Queen,
Mary Pickford and The Bombay Sapphire
he almost stole from The Smithsonian.

He'll play some Ravi Shankar, if alone,
but, even so, he can never tell if what he hears
is the evening raga

or the morning one. If the first martini
is the beginning of one thing,
or the welcome end of something else.

The Sitting

i.m. Basil Blackshaw

Northern southpaw,
leading with the right –
addressing the thing.
Some puzzle of tone perhaps,
or bad light.

Soutine comes up.
Kristofferson, Cézanne;
but mostly horses, badgers, greyhounds,
Staffordshire Bull Terriers
and a gleeful, outlaw plan for grub –

two local cuts of bloody steak
grilled on fresh-cut whins,
potatoes, butter, bit of salt,
Draught Guinness
in a can.

My place of total honour there –
that cushioned wooden chair.
The breath-taking slugs
of cobalt and red.
The two of us laughing.
Head to head.

Christmas Day

i.m. Dennis O'Driscoll

Such is the sun and unimagined snow,
that every downy fleck and tone glows
like decorations on the thorn.

All this magic so supposed to be,
the bauble bullfinch on a tree,
the fleeting, cocky wren.

Redwings make their runes and tracks.
Frantic chaffinches relax
and hop their private constellations on the lawn.

Only robins have a feel for sorrow.
In the holly they'll resume tomorrow.
Lament the tortured King.

Winter's Blessing

Unexpected birdsong
in the brief sun
of Sundays after Christmas
when you drink too much
and most miss the dead.

When you bow your head
to the soloing thrush,
lit like an old friend's soul
in the bones of a silver birch.

A Picture of a Bittern

It came home as a bookmark
in a signed *Collected Montague*.
The bittern. *An Bonnán Buí.*
Bought at the Brocante in Nice
as I killed an hour before the flight.

A colour plate – all raggedy and foxed –
the head-up, booming bird
sliced from an 1890s tome,
the bird itself already flown
from its black Fermanagh lakes.

So this was Héron Grand Butor –
Ardea dates the thing –
for now you'd write *Botaurus*, Ox and Bull.
A bhonnáin bhuí, 's é mo léan do luí,
'S do chnámha sínte tar éis do ghrinn.

I saw one stuffed in a poet's house –
stuffed and Sandymounted, you might say –
a bog-bull in a bell-jar, marble-eyed
in an airless afterlife.
What odds indeed about the end of Troy?

And while I've never heard its boom,
there's talk now of return,
the whole extinction not so absolute at all.
North Leitrim, no less. South Wexford.
And some day, maybe, Fermanagh and South Tyrone,

home to poets and the birds of golden rushes.
The Yellow Bittern and Cathal Buí – from own country –
and Montague in Nice, still there, walking by the prayer-halls
near Rue d'Angleterre. By Constantine's halls a bittern calls
from a wineless place.

By the Old County Hospital

When my father was a boy,
out by the old County Hospital,
he heard a screeching up ahead
that put the heart crossways in his chest.
Its frequency was razorblade and cruel –
the torture of an eyes-wide-open death.

In the shaken silence of its afterwards
a hawk was hunched on a fencepost,
a hawk that eyed him with its yellow eye
as it pulled apart some pulsing thing,
a sparrow that had chanced a flit
between one hedge and another.

My father was a worrier.
He would not forget that suffering bird,
the dreadful sonics of astonishment,
the unthinkable dismemberment,
the talon grip, the nipping beak.
The bloody morsels ripped away.

And then this morning, wandering,
there was a screeching up ahead
and the same bird had a magpie on the grass
(the female, being bigger, is capable of this)
and I heard for myself that crazed, insistent rasp
of terror and comprehension mixed.

It wouldn't stop until the throat was cut.
The hawk it nipped and picked and pulled
and held me with its yellow eye.

By the old County Hospital
my father watches it float along the hedge
towards the incinerator and the bins.

Headlights

He was tailed for hours that night.
This was Arizona –
beyond Flagstaff,
in the middle of nowhere.

It happened him in Belfast too,
and on a pitch-black road
in South Tyrone,
where one crowd let on to be the other.

He thought about his father and his mother.
He tried again to pray,
to make the headlights sweep
and turn away.

Following Mahler

He gets off at 72nd and makes for his glowing rooms
at the old Hotel Majestic.
But like the station, like the El, like the grand parade itself –
the one that roused the opening moments of the 5th –
the Majestic isn't there at all.

Sometimes, under Carnegie Hall, I stand
by his shoulder on the rattling train.
His breath is full of music, mine is caught with grief.
Call your mother, he says. *She'll be worried,*
and you so far from home.

I see the house, the hallway,
The creamy-coloured phone.
But like the station, like the El, like the grand parade itself –
the one that roused the opening moments of the 5th –
my mother isn't there at all.

3

Starlings

I watched them from the window in our new estate –
swarming on the aerials and chimney pots,
the block of garages, the asphalt roof with the horse's head,
the broken plastic hoops, the tyre-tubes and plates.

From the smuts and clouds they showered down,
stabbing at our little patch of lawn
as yet more gathered on the sills and fence-posts,
sending out songs that mimicked ringing phones,

sirens, even failed ignitions on the road.
Speckled. Iridescent. They hunched in hundreds
on clotheslines, mowers, handlebars,
the iron bins and concrete bunkers of the yard.

And so this morning in the Dublin suburbs,
on a shortcut through a big estate,
telephone lines hung with trainers like coats of arms
on the gates of a fallen pile, I felt at home

around the pebbledash and worn-out lawns,
the yellow weeds, the painted ugly words.
The old heart's dial twitching once again.
The wintry electronica of birds.

Pike

for Pat Lunny

Near Devenish, the boat tied sideways
to a golden screen that would cut the hand off you –
and yet was soft and featherheaded too –
I saw a scene in silhouette as unbelievable to me
as Viking ghosts or risen Christs.

A pike was plashing in the shallows –
out of its depth entirely – and a water-hen
was riding on its back, attacking fins and gills
and giving out yards in its own astonishment.
It was surely some mirage or wishful thought?

But then the trembling reeds began to part
and, just beneath the surface, the pike,
perplexed by impulse, emerged just inches from the boat
to hang there like a mottled log,
hints of wolfish gold and silver in the light.

With one hand I could have lifted it clear,
held it heavy and sky-high.
But with not a one to see it happen, I held instead
it's sinking misbelieving glare
as, slowly, I began to shimmer, rise and fly.

In paradisum

It could be Inishdoney on a summer's day
if it wasn't for the mad macaques,
and fruit bats as big as Benny's bus.

Or the dodo and the fody and the red-whiskered
bulbul (to be sung by McArdle
as *The Red-Whiskered Bulbul of Benmore*).

Beyond, in the pale shade,
I scoff *salade de christophine*
(we call it *chouchous*),

palm hearts and bitter gourd
(oh, always the bitter gourd)
as I quaff my Drostdy Hof.

And yonder is the tropicbird!
The cuckoo and the zebra dove.
The hare, the giant tortoise and the tang.

Two curlews thonder on the beach.
Bad weather on the sea. Vital signs of home
in the sunlit ogham of a coconut tree.

Rats

There's always rats, even at beauty spots
like Sandymount Strand,
where the trouser legs of Bloom shuddered
at the sight of Gerty's upper thighs.
Those rocks are rife with rats, and labyrinthine.

And that shop window in the first Arrondissement,
in Rue des Halles where dead rats hung
all-noosed as I wandered back to the Métro.
Every night I saw them gnawing upwards into death.
To a sweaty afterlife of trouser legs and flesh.

Snipe

The snipe
shot up and out
from under my boot –

sky-goat,
bog-rocket,
wind-chopping
zig-zagger.

All angles.
Harder to hit.

The Dipper

for Kate Ellen Rose

High water on the Abhainn Mhór.
And walking with you, my daughter,
caught between mizzle and downpour,
I likely explained that, according to Dinneen,
there are a million words in Irish for the rain.

That's the time we saw the dipper flail,
a day-time bat crash-landed in the flow,
and you loved the way it burrowed under
to go walk-about on polished stones.
This, it seems, unique among the passerines.

And the way it swims on flipper wings like fins,
more turtle-stroke than terrapin,
and we pictured then the underwater scene:
the jewelled plumage, bubbles made from sky,
the hook-jawed *Bradán Feasa* eye-to-eye.

Did I mention then its solid bones? The ouzel name
like *osle* (Old English for *an londubh buí)* but not the same.
Or that in Norway they have christened it the National Bird
and to my Oslo friends it's *fossekall* –
Old Man of the Waterfalls?

Here in Iar-Chonnacht it's *gabha dubh.*
Conamara. Granuaile. And you have to love
the way she had the measure of Queen Bess – Elizabeth I –
who addressed her properly in Iryshe no less,
then Greenwich Latin: *Cinclus cinclus* plus *hibernicus.*

But anyway. The rain tapped on the alder leaves.
The dark-stained bark, the moss, the yellow reeds
soft like a painter's wash. And all along the bank
we watched the dipper dive as she tried and tried and tried
for tiny gems of snails and grubs. The larvae of the caddis-fly.

The hut sat like a temple. A cobwebbed shrine to fishermen,
and we sheltered cosy at its holy gable end,
my daughter, my easy-going friend.
And no more questions then. No more instructive talk.
Just the rain, the constant river, and the risen dipper
    dipping on a rock.

Watching Cable News

We built our forts with hazel rods
and canopies of fern,
and sometimes a fire would be lit –
as fires have always been lit –
in a ring of blackened stones.
We'd sit together on the beaten clay.
Some smoked Woodbine. Some longed for rain.

Next day, you'd come upon the wreckage.
Enemy attack? Elephants on the rampage?
No. Just boys. Sometimes the same boys
who had built the thing, the same boys
who crushed the eggs of water hens
and tortured fish.

Even at the age of ten I would despair –
I'd curse humanity to Hell
and thrash the homeward hedges
with a broken switch.

The Sweep Returns

A tiny blackened Heracles,
pink as a girl around the eyes,

his element was smoke and soot,
the Hydra turfed in sections

in the Hades of his boot.
In the yard the Cretan Bull

was solid grief. Monumental
in our sacred Smokeless Zone.

Cerberus, monster cruel,
pirouetting sweetly for a bone.

From the Oxford Train

A man up to his oxters
in a blinding yellow field.
A kestrel too – a Hopkins bird
in England's atmosphere.

Then from the Isis, mesmerized,
a teal begins to climb,
taking several absent gradients
at the one transcendent time.

Nocturne

When I'm locking up at night,
checking everything twice, three times –
sometimes even more than that
as the mind slips and forgets the act
the instant it's complete –

I see her in the bungalow
at the very same routine, even though
the rooms are all in darkness now
and whatever fears she had are gone
like prayers or candle-smoke or song.

The alarm is set, the snib is on the door,
and yet my hand is once more on the handle –
pulling, pressing, ridiculously testing.
Like an old man trying to get out.
Or, already out, trying to get back in.

Studio Portraits

Harry Hudson, Darling Street,
the source of every picture.
Same spot. That prop a constant fixture
in all your different lives.

And there's resemblance right enough –
the mouth, the ears, the way I stand,
the way I hold my hands.
The image and the spit.

But while features in themselves are fine,
what else is there in any family's line?
Some trace of temperament perhaps?
Some sign of sadness, anger, joy, remorse?

Did any of you laugh out loud
when Harry Hudson
burrowed into his camera
like the arse-end of a pantomime horse?

Putting the Clocks Forward

The calculation throws me every time,
a simple sum a child could do but, even so,
the brain abandons me,

and suddenly I'm putting up a front.
I'm buying time, reckoning the future in my head
when all the children want to know

is will it mean an hour more or less in bed.
It's nothing, but I feel that jag of terror all the same.
Like when I can't remember who sang what.

Or, unaccountably,
I clean forget a boxer, an actor,
the local beauty's name.

The Van Der Voort Sisters

Sometimes in winter I enter the Park
and stand there in the frozen dark
just to watch them skate,

Rosetta and Janet, a long time dead,
perfecting their figures of eight
in bustles of purple and red.

I love their loops and arabesques.
I take my vodka from a silver flask.

What I Read Today

I read that the mother of Socrates was a midwife.
I read about Rauschenberg's *Erased de Kooning Drawing.*
I read a poem by Cavafy called *The Old Man.*
I read Tom Piazza's sleeve-notes for Dylan's *Triplicate.*
I read that Stockhausen's *Helicopter String Quartet*
requires four different airborne choppers.
I read the instructions for a NutriBullet,
an article about pigeons, the label on a wine bottle
and an email from a buddy on the road.
I read a ton of tweets, three DMs, a weather report,
two rumours and a letter from the bank.
I read a chapter of *The Radetsky March* by Joseph Roth.
I read that Hemingway wrote standing up
and that Dickens slept facing north.
I read a rejection letter that was very kindly put.
I read the ingredients on a soup tin,
the numbers on the clock and a press release from U2.
I read that Malcolm Arnold's *Grand Overture* op. 57
is scored for three electric vacuum cleaners, electric floor
    polishers,
four rifles and orchestra.
I read that Man Ray photographed the actual corpse of Proust.
I read that Fidel Castro was an extra in a movie called *Holiday
    in Mexico*
and that it starred Jane Powell and Walter Pidgeon.
I read the track-listing on the new Max Richter compilation.
I read the football results.
I read a text from Mick suggesting pints.
I read – in the shed – Richard Ford's *Between Them.*
I read words like Monteleone and Tucumcari.
On the online edition of *The Impartial Reporter*
I read my mother's obituary.

The Gymnast

for Amelia

When you cartwheel on the lawn,
even the swifts zoom in to marvel at your moves,

swifts that turn and flip and soar.
Perhaps the ones you've seen before in Spain?

Those evening, screeching ones
who anointed, twice, your ice-cream

with a little spits of ash –
by which I mean their shit –

as they flitted in and out of cracks
in leaning, restaurant walls.

There's luck in that, I said,
but you couldn't be convinced.

Not by me, or by the swifts.
Not by gravity or wit.

Now they watch you on the lawn,
perfecting acrobatics of your own.

A Twelve Mile Walk in September

Faithful, well able,
unbalanced only
by the views we leave behind,

we climb Mámean
to its bottomless tarn
and St. Patrick's certain bed.

New air. Quartzite.
Shining ravens on the move.
And ancient music, surely?

A gate of tubular steel
so perfectly holed that the wind
makes distant notes and chimes

that charm
and hold us still
between one thing

and another.
Black-faced sheep
and (up there somewhere)

white-tailed eagles
fit to float from here
to Donegal

in forty minutes flat.
If they don't get poisoned first.
Or shot.

To the other side a prairie,
all rolled out for buffalo.
And the one road earthwards

like a long
seductive finger
underneath the chin.

The shins are feeling it by now,
the steep descent to lusher lands
with climates of their own,

boreens flush with fuschia.
Blackberries full-exploding
on our tongues.

The ash is hung with berries too,
brash like earrings,
inedible but even so.

Then dragonflies rise.
Laughter from the schoolyard.
The sudden thrumming of our phones.

Across to Keane's for sandwiches
prepped like flowerbeds.
A funeral's aftermath –

people back from England.
Good suits, dresses, cigarettes.
We stretch, relax,

drink tea
and watch the swallows
host for Africa.

Our pot of blinding silver
as we sit there in the sun,
waiting for our lift to come –

the foot-down joy-ride
of accomplishment.
Back to square one.

The Metropolitan Museum of Art

for Evie at fifteen

There's a room in New York City,
and to stand on its threshold
is like entering Heaven,
or at least as Heaven was once explained to me,
loved ones gathered, old friends beaming,
all tippy-toed in welcome,
as excited by your sudden arrival
as you are yourself.

Or maybe –
just to leave Heaven out of it for now –
it's like a surprise birthday party
and everyone is overwhelmingly there:
all your treasured ones assembled,
some you haven't seen in years,
glimpsed already
in the corner of your eye.

Anyhow, I can tell you exactly where it is
and how to get there –
by subway, bus or yellow cab.
Or better still on foot,
the scenic route through Central Park.
I can scribble a map. I can tell you what's in store.
But, more and more, my darling girl,
I can only leave you to the door.

Weekend Away

The car slows for the turn,
for the ring-rumble
of a cattle grid.
Wheels greet gravel
and we're here.

We love this blessed threshold,
our hidden compound
with fossils in the doorstep,
where fishermen sip whiskey
and chat about the day:

Oh, he's a hard man on the rods.
Oh, Jesus, he's a hard man on the rods.
Goes for distance. He belts it out.

And oh, that echo on the wooden boards
as we head up to the room.
The big clattering key.
The cool sheets. The furnishings.
Our own invisibility.

We can run a bath.
Or run amok. Or both.
Or sit downstairs, for now,
and read our books. Hear the anglers'
talk of Silver Stoats and Gorgeous George

and how to gink him up.
Chowder and a pint perhaps.
Or look at maps of Derryclare and Maam.

Perhaps the mountains? Or an ice-cold swim?
It seems, love, that we can still do anything.

NOTES

'Lighting a Candle. St. Louis Cathedral, New Orleans' (p. 34) owes a debt to *The Gangs of New Orleans – An Informal History of The French Quarter Underworld* by Herbert Asbury (Arrow Books, 2004).

The last line of 'A Picture of a Bittern' (p. 53) is taken from Thomas MacDonagh's translation of *An Bonnán Buí* by Cathal Buí Mac Giolla Ghunna (c. 1680 – 1756).

The closing two lines of 'Chairman of The Board of Governors' (p. 39) are from 'The Winter Campaign' by Eochaidh Ó hEodhasa (c. 1565 – 1613). A prose rendering by Alan Harrison is included in *The Field Day Anthology of Irish Writing*, Volume 1: "Because of Maguire's circuit through the west of the land where the sun sets, there are *many courts in flames: no new destruction this, and many the land without heir or great-grandson*."